The Mayor of Casterbridge

A Story of a Man of Character

Thomas Hardy

Abridged and adapted by Phyllis Corzine

Illustrated by Jay Bensen

A PACEMAKER CLASSIC

GLOBE FEARON
Pearson Learning Group

Pacemaker Classics

The Adventures of Huckleberry Finn
The Adventures of Tom Sawyer
The Call of the Wild
A Christmas Carol
Crime and Punishment
David Copperfield
The Deerslayer
Dr. Jekyll and Mr. Hyde
Ethan Frome
Frankenstein
Great Expectations
Heart of Darkness
The Hunchback of Notre Dame
Jane Eyre
The Jungle Book
The Last of the Mohicans

The Mayor of Casterbridge
Moby Dick
The Moonstone
O Pioneers!
The Prince and the Pauper
The Red Badge of Courage
Robinson Crusoe
The Scarlet Letter
A Tale of Two Cities
The Three Musketeers
The Time Machine
Treasure Island
20,000 Leagues Under the Sea
Two Years Before the Mast
The War of the Worlds
Wuthering Heights

ISBN 0-8224-9342-X
Printed in the United States of America

9 10 VO88 10 09

Globe Fearon
Pearson Learning Group

1-800-321-3106
www.pearsonlearning.com

Contents

1 The Sale, the Oath, the Search

It was a late summer evening in the year 1830. A young man and woman were walking along a dusty road on the way to the village of Weydon-Priors. Both were dressed simply but not badly. The man was strong, dark, and stern looking. On his back he carried a basket of tools for cutting hay. The woman was plain. She was carrying a small baby girl in her arms. She plodded along as if time and chance might bring anything upon her—except fair play.

What was odd about the couple was the way they walked in perfect silence. At every step, the man ignored the woman. The woman seemed to expect this silence. She did not speak, either. Once in a while she would look down at the baby and smile. When she smiled at the baby, her face became pretty.

The hay cutter and his wife met a stranger as they neared town. "Is there any hay-cutting work here?" the young man asked.

The stranger said there was no work at all. "It's fair day," he added.

The young family kept going and soon came

upon the fairgrounds. The fair was just ending. The animal pens were empty; the best horses and sheep had already been sold. Yet the crowd was larger now than it had been in the morning. Everyone was enjoying the vendors, peep shows, toy stands, waxworks, and fortune-tellers.

The hay cutter and his wife did not care for those things, so they looked for something to eat or drink. The wife pointed to a tent with a sign that read, Good Furmity Sold Hear. They went in.

"I always like furmity," the wife said. "So does Elizabeth-Jane. And so will you."

"I've never tasted it," said the man. Then he learned that furmity was a thick, cooked liquid made from wheat, flour, milk, raisins, and other things. He ordered a bowl for himself and one for his wife. Then he winked at the hag who was making and selling the furmity, and she nodded back. With that she brought out a bottle of rum and poured some into his bowl.

The hay cutter decided that he liked furmity. That is, he liked the way the old hag had fixed it up for him. He had several more bowls, though this was making his wife uneasy.

The wife said over and over, "Michael, let's go find some lodgings."

The man ignored his wife and his tired child. Instead, he kept eating. After his first bowl of furmity, he was still himself. After his second, he became jolly. After his third, he began to argue with people; and after his fourth, he became rude.

"I married at 18, like a fool," he said. "Now this is all I have." He pointed at himself and his family. At the same time, he could hear a man outside selling the last of the old horses at the fair.

"Men who have wives and don't want them should be able to get rid of them like those old horses," he went on. "I'd sell mine this minute if anybody would buy her!"

At first, people thought the man was joking. But his wife was angry.

"Michael, a joke is a joke," she said. "But you may make it once too often."

"I know I've said it before," he said. "But I meant it. All I want is five guineas." Then the man had another bowl of furmity, with more rum in it.

"Will anybody buy my wife?" he asked the others in the tent. "She can take the child and go her own way. I'll take my tools and go my way. Does anybody want her? Yes or no?"

"Yes," said a loud voice from the doorway. All eyes turned. Standing there was a sailor.

"You say you do?" asked the husband.

"I say so," answered the sailor.

"Where is your money?"

The sailor took out five clean bills and threw them

on the table. "I want her only if she is willing," he said calmly. "I don't want to hurt her feelings."

"She is willing if she can take the child," said the husband. "She said so the other day."

"Do you swear?" the sailor asked her.

The woman looked at her husband. He didn't look at all sorry. "I swear," she said to the sailor. Then she turned to the hay cutter and flung her wedding ring in his face.

"Michael," she said, "I am no longer yours. I'll try my luck somewhere else. It will be better for me and for Elizabeth-Jane, too." She took the sailor's arm and left with him, sobbing.

It was late then, so the rest of the crowd began leaving as well. With that, the man simply put his head down on the table and went to sleep. The furmity woman couldn't wake him, so she left him where he slept.

The next morning the man awoke with the sun shining into the tent. As he looked around, he saw something shiny on the ground. He picked it up; it was his wife's wedding ring. Then he put his hand in his pocket and felt the money. Only then did he remember what had happened the night before.

"Did I tell my name to anybody last night?" he asked to himself. He decided that he had not. Then he thought of his wife. He was surprised and annoyed that she was gone. "She must have thought

the sale was legal," he thought to himself. He knew that she was a simple woman.

Then the man shouted, "Blast her! Why did she go? She knew I was not in my right mind!"

With that, the man started walking down the road to find his wife. As he walked, he began to feel ashamed of himself. When he came to a town with a church, he went inside and made the following promise: "I, Michael Henchard, take an oath before God that I will not drink any strong liquor for 21 years. That is a year without liquor for every year I have lived. May I be struck dumb, blind, and helpless if I break this oath."

With that done, Henchard began searching again for his wife and child. He could not even find out the name of the sailor who had taken her away. It wasn't long before the days began to add up to weeks. Then the weeks began to add up to months. Still he searched on. Of course, he didn't tell people how he had lost his wife. He was too ashamed.

Finally Henchard gave up his hopeless search. He decided instead to settle in one place. He chose to go to the town of Casterbridge, in a far distant part of Wessex.

2 Eighteen Years Later

The road into Weydon-Priors was still covered with dust. Two women, both dressed in black, were walking along the road. One had been Michael Henchard's young wife, Susan. Now she was much older. The other, about 18, was Michael and Susan Henchard's grown-up daughter.

"Why do we waste our time coming here?" asked the girl.

"My dear Elizabeth-Jane, this is where I first met Newson," explained her mother.

"You first met Father here? Oh yes, you have told me so before. And now he's drowned and gone from us!"

"Also, this was the last place where I saw the relative we are now looking for—Mr. Michael Henchard," said her mother.

"How is he related to us, Mother?"

"He is, or was—for he may be dead—a relative by marriage," said her mother.

As they walked toward the fairgrounds, the mother noticed a ragged old woman stooped over a cooking pot. "Good furmity sold here!" called the old woman.

The mother remembered the woman. "I will just say a word to her. Elizabeth-Jane, you stay here."

Making sure that her daughter could not hear her, Susan Henchard asked the old woman, "Do you remember when a man sold his wife in your tent 18 years ago today?"

The old woman did remember. "He came back here the next year," said the old woman. "He asked about his wife. Then he said he was going to Casterbridge. He told me to tell anyone who asked."

Susan Henchard thanked her and returned to Elizabeth-Jane. "I think we'll go to Casterbridge," she said.

Henchard's wife had tried to do what was right. She had almost told Elizabeth-Jane the truth a hundred times. But she never did tell her. The girl grew up believing that her mother and Newson were a normal married couple.

Susan Henchard was a very simple woman. For a long time, she had believed she was Newson's legal wife. However, after many years, Susan told a friend about her past. The friend laughed and told Susan she was not legally married to Newson. Susan then felt ashamed of her life with Newson. She told him she didn't know if she could live with him any longer.

When the season came, Newson left home for a sailing trip to Newfoundland. Soon after, Susan received word that he had been lost at sea. She and her daughter lived on in the cottage, making nets for fishermen.

Soon Elizabeth-Jane began to reach womanhood. The sight of her daughter made Susan sad. Elizabeth-Jane had the makings of a great beauty. Yet she would not have a chance to become beautiful unless she got out of the grips of poverty. At last Susan decided to search for Henchard. She hoped that he would help care for his beautiful daughter.

The two women arrived in the outskirts of Casterbridge on a Friday evening at dusk. They overheard two men talking. One of them said Henchard's name. Elizabeth-Jane wanted to run after the men and ask about Henchard.

"No, no, no! Not just yet," said her mother. "He may be in jail for all we know."

When the women arrived in Casterbridge, they were hungry. Susan Henchard asked some women where the nearest baker was. "You can't get good bread in Casterbridge these days," said one of the women. "Our bakers have bought bad wheat. The loaves of bread are as flat as toads."

Susan and Elizabeth-Jane walked on. Soon they heard a brass band playing in front of the best hotel in Casterbridge, the King's Arms. A group of people had gathered in front of the hotel. Susan felt it was a good place to ask about Henchard.

"Elizabeth-Jane, you had better be the one to do it," said her mother.

Elizabeth-Jane walked up to an old man in the crowd. "What's going on here tonight?" she asked. The old man said it was a dinner party, given by Mayor Henchard.

"Henchard!" exclaimed Elizabeth-Jane.

Meanwhile, a 40-year-old man was seating himself inside the hotel dining room. He was at the head of the table, facing the windows. He had a strong body and a large face. His voice was strong as well. He had flashing black eyes and dark, bushy hair. The man was dressed in an evening suit and wore a heavy gold chain. His name was Michael Henchard.

To Susan's surprise, the three wine glasses next to his plate were empty. He was drinking water.

"Do you see him, mother?" whispered the girl.

"Yes, yes," answered Susan. "Now I want to go."

"Doesn't he seem likely to be a friend to us?" asked Elizabeth-Jane. "I think he looks like a generous man. Why do you feel so afraid of him? I'm not at all. I'll call upon him. He can only say he won't accept such distant relations."

"I don't think I can ever meet Mr. Henchard," replied Susan.

"Just wait a little," said Elizabeth-Jane. She turned her attention to Henchard and the old man at her elbow.

"Don't they fill Mr. Henchard's glass?" Elizabeth-Jane asked the old man.

"Ah, no. He never touches nothing. I heard that he swore a gospel oath in past years. He's got two more years to go, they say.

"He's the most powerful member of the town council," the man added. "And he's important in the countryside, too. Henchard's got a hand in all the wheat, oats, hay, and such around here. This year he got some bad grain, though. I've never tasted such rough bread before."

The band then struck up another song. When it was over, Henchard told a funny story about his grain business. Everyone laughed heartily until a

11

voice from the crowd spoke up.

"This is all very well. But how about the bad bread?" asked the voice from the crowd.

Henchard answered. "Well, I know the wheat turned out bad," he said. "I didn't mean to buy and sell bad wheat. I have found my business is too large to handle myself. I'm going to hire a manager so that these mistakes will not happen."

Henchard went on. "If anybody could tell me how to turn bad wheat into good wheat, I'd take the wheat back. But it can't be done." With that, Henchard sat down.

3 Henchard and Farfrae

In the meantime, another stranger had joined the crowd outside. He was a good-looking young man carrying a suitcase. He had a small build, a reddish complexion, and bright eyes.

When this man heard Henchard's closing words, "It can't be done," he smiled. Then he quickly wrote a note, folded it, and handed it to a waiter inside. "Give this to the mayor at once," he said.

Elizabeth-Jane liked the sound of the young man's voice. He seemed to be a Scotchman. She heard him ask someone in the crowd for the name of a hotel that was less costly than the King's Arms.

"They say the Three Mariners is a very good place," he was told. Then the young man walked off in the direction of the Three Mariners.

Elizabeth-Jane and her mother also needed a place to stay the night. "Let's go where the young man has gone," Elizabeth-Jane said to her mother. Her mother agreed.

Just after the two women left, Mayor Henchard stepped out into the street. He was looking for the young man who had sent him the note. He learned that the young man had gone to the Three Mariners, so he walked off in that direction.

Susan and Elizabeth-Jane stood outside the Three Mariners for a moment. It was a modest inn. Still they feared it might cost too much. Finally they went in. The landlord led them to a small room upstairs. It was clean and well kept.

Susan Henchard quickly shouted, "It is too good for us!"

"I am afraid so, too," said Elizabeth-Jane. "But we must be respectable.

"I know what I'll do!" said Elizabeth-Jane. She then left the room and made her way to the bar. There she found the landlady sitting on a bar stool.

"You seem very busy, tonight" said Elizabeth-Jane. "My mother and I are not well-off. May I pay our way by helping out tonight?"

The landlady was surprised at this old-fashioned offer. Yet she agreed to let Elizabeth work that night.

Elizabeth-Jane and her mother happened to get the room next to the young Scotchman's. The wall between the rooms was very thin. They could hear the Scotchman talking with Mayor Henchard!

"Are you the one who answered my ad for the manager's job?" asked Henchard.

"No," said the Scotchman, surprised.

"Surely you are the man," said Henchard. "Joshua, Jipp . . . Jopp . . . What was his name?"

"My name is Donald Farfrae. I am in the grain

business, but I am on my way to Bristol, and from there I shall go to America."

"Well, well," said Henchard.

The two men continued to talk. Farfrae explained to Henchard how to make the bad wheat taste better. Henchard was very happy with the news.

The mayor said, "If you'll work for me, you can manage the wheat business alone. And I'll pay you well."

"You're very kind, but I cannot," said Mr. Farfrae. "My plans are fixed."

Henchard found that he liked the young Scotchman very much. "Well, I shall get a manager somewhere," said Henchard. "But I won't find one I like as well!"

Henchard then left, and Farfrae joined the other hotel guests downstairs. Farfrae made himself at home. Soon he began singing Scottish songs. People gathered around him to listen.

Elizabeth-Jane heard the lovely singing as she worked that night. She had never heard anything like it. Neither had the other guests. No one spoke or drank. They were all too busy listening. The crowd clapped loudly at the end of each song. They asked Farfrae to sing again and again.

After more singing and talking, Donald Farfrae said that he had to go to his room and get some sleep. Elizabeth-Jane quickly sneaked upstairs to

turn down his bed. She blushed upon meeting him in the hallway. He sang some words about a beautiful lass. Then Elizabeth-Jane flew to her room, full of thoughts about Donald Farfrae.

The next morning Elizabeth-Jane flung open the window. The cool air had the smell of fall in it. As she looked out, she saw Henchard walking up the street. Farfrae was leaning out of his window.

"You are leaving soon, I suppose?" Henchard called to Farfrae.

"Yes, almost this moment, sir."

"Then shall we walk together to the edge of town?" asked Henchard.

"If you'll wait a minute," answered the Scotchman. A moment later he was outside.

"You should have taken the job," said Henchard.

"Yes, yes, perhaps it would've been wiser," said Donald.

Elizabeth-Jane then turned back into the room. "He was a good man—and now he's gone," she said to herself sadly.

During breakfast, Elizabeth-Jane and her mother talked about Henchard. Finally, Mrs. Henchard decided to send Mr. Henchard a note. The note said that Henchard's relative, Susan, a sailor's widow, was in town. She would let him decide whether or not to see her.

Mrs. Henchard gave Elizabeth-Jane the note. "If he thinks he's too important to see us, then tell him we will quietly leave Casterbridge," she said.

"And if he says yes?" asked Elizabeth-Jane.

"Then tell him to send a note saying when and how he will meet me."

Elizabeth-Jane went off to Henchard's place of business. She knocked on the door, and someone called, "Come in."

She turned the handle, and there stood the young Scotchman, Donald Farfrae! He looked as if he belonged there. His hat was hung on a hook. His suitcase was in the corner. Elizabeth-Jane was so surprised she could not speak at first.

"Yes, what is it?" asked the Scotchman. He didn't recognize her at all. Disappointed, Elizabeth-Jane murmured that she wanted to see Mr. Henchard.

"Yes. Will you wait a moment? He's busy just now." Farfrae showed her to a chair and then turned back to his work.

While Elizabeth-Jane sits waiting, we may explain how Farfrae came to Mr. Henchard's office.

That morning Henchard walked with Donald to the edge of town. Before he turned back, he stopped.

"Now I am not a man to lose out," said Henchard. "Before you are gone forever, I'll ask once more. Will you stay?"

The young man looked out over the country. Then he looked back along the shaded walk toward town.

"I never expected this—I did not!" he said. "It must be God's will. I will not go to America. I'll stay and be your man." The two men shook hands.

"Done," said Henchard.

"Done," said Donald Farfrae.

Then Henchard showed Farfrae his barns and his office. And it was in his office that Elizabeth-Jane had found Farfrae.

4   A New Start

After some time Elizabeth-Jane was finally let into Henchard's office.

"Now then, what is it, young woman?" asked Henchard.

"I am sent to tell you, sir, that a distant relation of yours is in town. Her name is Susan Newson. She is a sailor's widow."

Henchard's face turned a little red. "Oh, Susan is . . . still alive?"

"Yes, sir."

"Are you her daughter?"

"Her only daughter," answered Elizabeth-Jane.

"What . . . is your name?"

"Elizabeth-Jane, sir."

"Newson?" he asked.

"Elizabeth-Jane Newson," she answered.

Henchard knew from her answer that Susan had not told Elizabeth-Jane about her past. It was more than he had expected. His wife had acted kindly to him in return for his unkindness.

Henchard showed Elizabeth-Jane out of the office, through the garden, and into his house.

"Sit down, Elizabeth-Jane. Your mother is well?"

"She is tired," answered Elizabeth-Jane.

"A sailor's widow," Henchard thought. "When did your father die?" he asked.

"Father was lost last spring."

They talked for a while. Then Henchard sat down at the table and wrote a letter. He put the note and some money in an envelope and gave it to Elizabeth-Jane.

"Give this letter to your mother, please," said Henchard. "I am glad to see you here, Elizabeth-Jane," he said warmly. Elizabeth-Jane was touched by his kindness.

She returned to the inn and gave her mother the letter. Susan asked her daughter to describe the meeting. Then she finally opened the letter.

> Meet me at eight o'clock tonight, if you can, at the Ring, on Budmouth Road. The place is easy to find. I can say no more now. The news upsets me. Don't tell the girl anything until I have seen you.
>
> M. H.

He had said nothing about the money. Susan noticed that it was exactly five guineas—the amount Mr. Newson had paid for her. It seemed that Henchard was buying her back again.

The Ring was an ancient arena in Casterbridge, built by the Romans nearly two thousand years ago. It was a lonely, sad place, with an unhappy past. Roman prisoners had once fought wild animals there. Years later it was where criminals were hanged. Many people had died in that place. Often people thought they saw ghosts there.

Henchard was already there when Susan reached the Ring. Neither spoke at first. The poor woman leaned against Henchard, and he held her in his arms.

"I don't drink," he said in a low voice. "You hear, Susan? I don't drink now. I haven't had a drink since that night." Those were his first words.

They talked for a long while. Henchard explained that he had thought she was dead and gone.

"Why did you keep silent like this?" he asked.

Susan told him she had thought she belonged to Newson.

"Elizabeth-Jane cannot be told," he said. "She would hate us both. I could not bear it!"

"That's why I never told her about you." Susan replied. "I could not bear it either."

Susan and Michael Henchard talked about what to do. "I don't see how you both can return to my house as the wife and daughter I once treated badly," said Henchard.

"We'll go away at once. I only came to see . . ."

"No, no, Susan. You are not to go," he said kindly.

Henchard explained his plan. "You and Elizabeth take a house in town as the widow Mrs. Newson and her daughter. I'll pay the costs. I meet you, we begin to see each other, and then we marry.

"Elizabeth-Jane can become my stepdaughter," he added. "This would keep my old life a secret. Only you and I would know."

Susan agreed to Henchard's plan. "I like the idea of marrying again," she said. "It seems the right thing to do. Now I must go back to Elizabeth-Jane and tell her that you wish us to stay in town." Mrs. Henchard walked back to town alone.

When Henchard returned home, he found Donald Farfrae still working at the office. He invited his new partner to dinner. Over dinner, Henchard told Farfrae the story of his past. He explained how he had sold his wife and child. He had never told anyone that story before.

"And now she has come back," he said. "This very morning."

"Can you take her back to live with you?" asked Farfrae.

Henchard said that that was his plan. "But, Farfrae," he added sadly, "when I do the right thing for Susan, I will wrong another woman."

Henchard went on to tell Farfrae about another woman whom he often visited in Jersey. She had taken care of him when he was sick. Henchard explained that she was not careful about how things looked to others. People had the wrong idea about them.

"She has suffered much because of me," he said. "And she hasn't forgotten to tell me so in one letter after another." Henchard went on, "I must say I meant to marry her. I told her that if Susan was not alive (and I believed she was not), then I would marry her. But now, Susan appears."

"You must write to the young lady," said Farfrae, "and explain that she cannot be your wife."

After Farfrae left, Henchard sent a letter and some

money to the other woman.

"Can it be so easy?" he asked. "Now then, to see Susan."

Henchard began visiting Susan often. People began to notice and whisper that the mayor of Casterbridge might soon be married. But no one could understand his choice. The mayor had never noticed women before. Now he was paying attention to this humble woman. Susan was so pale that the town boys called her "the ghost."

Henchard was not bothered by the talk. He just wanted to make up to Susan for what he had done. He also wanted to give Elizabeth-Jane a nice home. Henchard also felt that marrying such a poor, plain woman would be a just punishment for what he had done.

When the wedding day arrived, townspeople stood outside the church talking about the pair.

"Daze me! I never saw a man wait so long to take so little!" said one man.

"I wouldn't wish for a better man," said a woman. "But there is something strange about all this. It will come out in time."

5 Fortunes Change

Mrs. Henchard and Elizabeth-Jane moved into the mayor's large, roomy house. Their poverty and suffering were over. Henchard was as kind to them as he could be. He gave Elizabeth-Jane anything she wanted, and it made a great change in her.

As the winter and spring passed, Elizabeth-Jane's thin face and figure filled out. Her paleness disappeared, and her face became brighter. She was quickly becoming a pretty young woman. Henchard came to love her as his daughter, and she often went walking with him.

One day Henchard and his wife were at breakfast, talking about Elizabeth-Jane. "Now Susan," he said, "I want to have her called Miss Henchard—not Miss Newson. I don't like the other name at all. I'll have a notice put in the Casterbridge newspaper."

"No. Oh, no. But . . ." said Susan.

"Well, I shall do it," he said. "Surely if she is willing, you must wish it as much as I do."

Later Susan went to Elizabeth-Jane to tell her about the name change. "Isn't it a bit like forgetting Newson—now that he's dead and gone?" asked Susan.

"I'll think about it," Elizabeth-Jane answered.

Nothing more was said of it, and nothing was done. Elizabeth still called herself Miss Newson.

Meanwhile, Henchard's business affairs improved under Donald Farfrae's direction. Donald and Henchard became good friends, and Henchard treated Farfrae like a younger brother.

One day Elizabeth-Jane got a note asking her to go to Durnover Hill, where Henchard kept wheat and hay. The note was not signed. She went there and waited.

Soon she saw Donald Farfrae coming toward her. He, too, was expecting someone. Could it be she? If so, why?

"Ah, it is Miss Newson," he said as he saw her. "I have come as you asked."

"Oh, Mr. Farfrae," she said. "So have I. But I didn't know it was you who wished to see me."

"I wished to see you? Oh, no. That is, I am afraid there has been some mistake."

"Didn't you ask me to come here?" asked Elizabeth-Jane. "Didn't you write this?" She held out her note.

"No, I didn't," he said. "But didn't you write this?" He held up his note.

"By no means," she replied.

"Then it's somebody who wants to see us both. Perhaps we should wait a little longer."

They waited and talked awhile. When no one

came, Elizabeth-Jane left. As he watched her walk away, Farfrae again whistled one of his happy old Scottish songs.

Elizabeth-Jane was becoming more beautiful every day. Donald Farfrae noticed it, too. But even though Henchard would buy her as many pretty clothes as she wanted, she was still careful about her dress. She did not want to attract too much attention. She was still a kind and quiet girl. For her, books and learning were more important than anything else.

One morning Henchard became angry with Abel Whittle, one of his workmen who was late again. Abel was always late for work, holding up the others. Henchard wanted to teach Abel a lesson. He went to his house.

"Out of bed, sir, and off to work," Henchard shouted. "March on! Never mind your pants."

Poor Abel ran to work without his pants on. He was blushing with shame.

When he got there, Donald Farfrae looked at him, amazed.

"Get back home and slip on your pants. Come to work like a man," he ordered.

Abel answered, "But Mr. Henchard said . . ."

"I don't care what Mr. Henchard said—or anybody else," said Donald.

Henchard saw Abel leaving. "Who's sending him back?" he shouted. All the men looked toward Farfrae.

"I am," said Donald. "I say this joke has been carried far enough."

"And I say it hasn't!" said Henchard. "Get up in the wagon, Whittle."

"Not if I am manager," said Donald. "He either goes home or I leave this place for good," said Donald.

Henchard looked at him, his face turning red. But he stopped for a moment. Donald went up to him.

"Come," said Donald quietly. "A man like you should know better. This is not like you."

"Why did you speak to me like that in front of the men?" asked Henchard. His voice was hurt and bitter. "You might have waited until we were alone. Oh, I know why. I told you the secret of my life. Now you think you can treat me as you will."

"I had forgotten it," Donald answered.

Henchard looked at the ground, said nothing more, and turned away. Later that day Donald learned something else about his boss. Henchard had helped Abel's mother every winter by sending her coal for heating fuel. He was not so hard or mean as he seemed. Still, the workers now thought Donald Farfrae was the better man.

Afterward Donald told Henchard he was sorry.

They became friends again. But Henchard began to worry about the secret he had told Farfrae. As he worried, he became cooler toward him. He no longer asked Farfrae to dinner.

Life went on. A holiday was coming, but Mayor Henchard had made no plans for it. Then Donald Farfrae asked Henchard if he could borrow his canvas cloths. He was planning a town picnic for the holiday.

"Have as many cloths as you like," Henchard said.

Henchard decided that he, too, should hold a picnic for the holiday. Donald was going to charge people who came to his picnic. Therefore Henchard decided that his picnic would be free.

When the holiday came, the weather was rainy and windy. Few people went to Henchard's picnic even though it cost nothing. Toward the end of the day, the rain stopped. Henchard thought that then he could at least hold a dance. But only two men and a woman showed up.

"Where are all the people?" Henchard asked one of the men. "The shops are all closed. Why don't they come?"

"They are at Farfrae's picnic," the man answered.

Henchard finally gave up his plans. He walked toward Farfrae's picnic and dance. He was surprised to find that the cloths he had given Farfrae had been used to make a large tent. It seemed that the whole town was there, even Susan and Elizabeth-Jane.

Henchard overheard people saying what a good idea the tent was. He heard how much the people liked Donald and how Henchard should learn from the things Donald did. Then Henchard saw Elizabeth-Jane dancing with Farfrae. It seemed everyone wanted to be with Farfrae instead of him!

Henchard decided to fire Donald. He announced, "Mr. Farfrae's time as my manager is coming to an end, isn't it, Farfrae?"

Donald quietly nodded his head.

People quickly asked Farfrae why he was no longer working for Henchard. He simply replied that Mr. Henchard no longer needed his help.

Henchard then went home. Elizabeth-Jane left the dance shortly after Henchard. Farfrae followed her.

"May I walk on with you as far as your street corner?" he asked. As they walked together he said, "I'm going to leave you soon."

"Why?" she asked, surprised.

"Oh, just business. But it is for the best."

Elizabeth-Jane let out an unhappy sigh.

"I wish I were richer, Miss Newson," Farfrae said. "I wish your stepfather were not angry. I would ask you something in a short time. I would ask you tonight!"

Farfrae never said what he would have asked her. Elizabeth-Jane was silent, afraid to ask. They parted.

Farfrae went back the way he had come, and Elizabeth-Jane went up the street toward her home.

In the morning, when he was no longer jealous and angry, Henchard felt sorry for what he had done. He was even more upset when he learned that Farfrae was going to take him at his word.

It became quickly known in Casterbridge that Farfrae and Henchard had parted ways. Elizabeth-Jane was worried about whether Farfrae would leave town. At last news reached her that he'd decided not to leave town after all.

Farfrae had bought a business, the same kind of business as Henchard's. Elizabeth-Jane was happy, but Henchard was angry at the news.

"He came here without a good shoe to his foot!" he told friends. "Didn't I offer him a living? Didn't I give him money and whatever he wanted? Now look what he's done to me! Well, I'll show him that I can do business better than a skinny newcomer!"

Not all of the local businessmen felt as Henchard did. For one thing, Henchard was not as popular as he had once been. His amazing energy had been good for business. However, he had made some people look bad along the way.

At home one night, Henchard decided to speak with Elizabeth-Jane. When she saw his face, she looked alarmed.

"There is nothing to worry about, dear," he said.

"I just want to know. Have you made any promises to Farfrae?"

"No. I have promised him nothing," said Elizabeth-Jane.

"Good. Then I wish you not to see him again."

"Very well, sir."

"You promise?"

She stopped a moment, then said, "Yes, if you wish it."

"I do. He is an enemy to our house!"

When she had gone, Henchard wrote a note to Farfrae telling him not to see Elizabeth-Jane again. One would have thought that Henchard would be glad to have Farfrae as a son-in-law. But Henchard was too stubborn to buy out a rival in that way.

Meanwhile, Farfrae did well in his business. He was careful not to take business away from Henchard. Still, Farfrae's business increased. Luck probably had nothing to do with it. "Character is fate," said the writer Novalis. And Farfrae was everything Henchard was not.

Nearly every Saturday, Henchard and Farfrae ran into each other in the market. Donald was always ready to say a few friendly words. Yet the Mayor always looked right past him. And anytime Susan would speak about Farfrae, Henchard would say, "What, are you against me, also?"

6 Elizabeth-Jane on Her Own

Before long a situation occurred in the Henchard household that would change the lives of everyone. It was something Elizabeth-Jane had expected for some time. Her mother was sick—too sick to leave her room. Henchard sent for the richest and busiest doctors he could find. (He thought they must have been the best.) After a day or two, Susan seemed better.

The next morning, when Henchard sat down to breakfast, he was surprised to find a letter from Jersey. He knew the handwriting—too well. He opened the letter and began to read it.

The writer said that she knew she could not see him now that he was married. She was not angry. She, too, wanted to keep their past a secret. She asked only that Henchard give back all the letters she had sent him. Her letter went on:

> I am now on my way to Bristol. I am going to see my only relative. She is rich, and I hope she will do something for me. I will pass through Casterbridge on my way. Can you meet me with the

letters at half past five on Wednesday
at the Antelope Hotel?

Lucetta

"Poor thing!" thought Henchard. "It would have been better if you had not known me! If ever I were able to marry you, I should do it."

Henchard knew how sick Susan was, and he was thinking about her death.

Henchard packed up the letters and went to meet Lucetta at the time and place she had suggested. But when she never arrived, he gave up and went home. He was glad he had not seen her.

Meanwhile, Mrs. Henchard was getting sicker. She could not go out at all. One day she asked for a pen and paper and then asked to be left alone. She wrote a letter and sealed it. On the outside she wrote these words: *Mr. Michael Henchard. Not to be opened until Elizabeth-Jane's wedding day.*

Elizabeth-Jane sat up with her mother night after night. One night Susan asked her about Farfrae.

"I got him to meet you at Durnover Hill," Susan said. "It was not to trick you. I did it to bring you together."

"Why?" asked Elizabeth-Jane, surprised.

"I . . . wanted you to marry Mr. Farfrae."

A few days later Farfrae was passing Henchard's house, and he saw the curtains closed. He rang the bell softly. He was told that Mrs. Henchard was dead. She had died that very hour.

Three weeks after Mrs. Henchard's death, Elizabeth-Jane and Henchard sat talking by the fireplace. Henchard was feeling alone. He had lost his friend Farfrae, then his wife. Elizabeth-Jane was the only person close to him. As he looked at her, he could no longer keep his secret.

"What did your mother tell you about me, about my past?" he asked.

"That you were related by marriage."

"She should have told you more, before you knew me! Then this would not be so hard to say. Elizabeth, I am your father, not Richard Newson."

Elizabeth was very still.

Henchard went on to explain that he and Susan had been married when they were young. But he did not tell Elizabeth-Jane the whole truth. He told her that Susan thought he was dead, and that was why she had married Newson.

Elizabeth-Jane became upset and began crying.

"Don't cry!" said Henchard. "I'll do anything if only you will look upon me as your father!"

She wanted to trust him. But for some reason she did not feel right.

"I don't want you to love me all of a sudden," said Henchard. "I'll show you papers to prove I am telling

the truth. It was I who chose your name. Your mother wanted it to be Susan."

Henchard started to leave the room but came back. "One word more," he said. "Will you take my name now? Your mother was against it, but it is yours, you know. Let me put a few lines in the newspaper announcing that Henchard is to be your name."

"If it is my name, I must have it, mustn't I?" she asked. "I wonder why Mother didn't wish it?"

Henchard quickly got a pen and paper and wrote a notice for the Casterbridge newspaper. The note said that Elizabeth-Jane Newson was going to call herself Elizabeth-Jane Henchard. He quickly sent the letter off to be published.

"Now," said Henchard, "I'll go upstairs and find some papers that will prove it all to you. Good night, my Elizabeth-Jane!"

As Henchard hunted for the papers, he found the letter that Susan had written before she died. The letter was not sealed well, and it fell open. He could not help reading it.

> My Dear Michael,
> For the good of all three of us, I have kept one thing a secret. Elizabeth-Jane is not your Elizabeth-Jane—the child who was in my arms when you sold me. No. Our child died three months after that. This living child is my other husband's. I gave her the same name to fill up the loss I felt. I hope you can forgive me.
>
> Susan Henchard

Henchard sat silently for a long time. Now he knew why his wife had not wanted Elizabeth-Jane to change her name. He walked into Elizabeth-Jane's room and watched her sleeping. Now he could see that she looked like Newson. Suddenly he could not stand the sight of her.

Henchard decided to let Elizabeth-Jane continue

to believe that she was his daughter. He could not bear the shame of telling her the truth.

The next morning Elizabeth-Jane came downstairs to breakfast and took Henchard by the arm. "I have thought all night," she said. "You have done so much for me! Mr. Newson was very kind, but that is not the same as having a real father." And she kissed Henchard on the cheek.

It was the moment he had been waiting for. Yet now it meant nothing to him. From that time on, Henchard was changed. He was cold and distant to Elizabeth-Jane. He began eating out with his friends instead of staying home with her. He even said unkind things about the way she talked.

Elizabeth-Jane did not complain about the unkindness. She was simply hurt. Her father seemed to love her less and less.

In the meantime Henchard's time as mayor was ending. He learned that he would not be asked to be mayor again. There was even a chance that Farfrae would take his place. This made Henchard even angrier.

He thought about how his life had changed. Ever since his wife and her daughter had come to Casterbridge, his luck had gone bad. That dinner at the King's Arms had been the high point of his life. Things seemed to fall apart after that.

Henchard wished he were free of Elizabeth-Jane.

He could no longer stand to see her. One evening he was thinking of Farfrae and how he had told Farfrae to stop seeing Elizabeth-Jane. Suddenly he had an idea. He jumped up with excitement. "He'll think it means peace and a marriage," he thought. "He will never guess I don't want her in my house any longer."

He wrote Farfrae a letter telling him to visit Elizabeth-Jane if he wished. His hope was that Farfrae would marry her.

The next morning Elizabeth-Jane visited her mother's grave. As she sat on a bench near the grave, she was feeling very sad, and she said aloud, "Oh, I wish I were dead with dear Mother!"

To her surprise, a young woman leaned over the bench. She was a stranger, very pretty and beautifully dressed.

"Yes, I heard you," said the woman. "What has happened?"

The two talked for awhile, and at last Elizabeth-Jane told the woman what had happened since her mother had died. The woman listened kindly.

"It sounds as if your father has a bad temper," said the woman. "But he is not a bad man."

"Oh no, he is not bad," said Elizabeth-Jane. She thought it strange that the woman seemed to side with her while not saying anything unkind about Henchard.

Elizabeth-Jane told the woman the story of her life as she knew it. Her new friend was not surprised.

"I don't want to go back to that house," said Elizabeth-Jane. "But what can I do? Where can I go?"

"I would like somebody to live in my house and keep me company," said the woman. "Would you come to live with me?"

"Oh, yes!" cried Elizabeth-Jane, with tears in her eyes. "I would do anything to get away. Perhaps then my father might again love me. But where do you live?"

"I am moving into High-Place Hall today. It is the old stone house that looks down over the market," said the woman. "Now think this over and meet me here the first fine day next week to give me your answer."

Elizabeth smiled joyfully, and the two parted.

That evening Elizabeth-Jane walked to High-Place Hall. It was a large stone house near the middle of town. Elizabeth-Jane saw lights in the upper rooms. The lady had already moved in. Then as Elizabeth-Jane turned to leave, she heard footsteps. She did not want anyone to see her, so she hurried off.

If Elizabeth-Jane had stayed, she would have been surprised. The person whom she had heard coming was Henchard. They did not see each other.

Henchard arrived home shortly after Elizabeth-Jane did. The girl quickly asked, "Father, do you mind if I go away for some time?"

"Go away? No, not at all. Where are you going?"

"I have a chance to go to a place where I can study and learn more."

"Then make the best of it," answered Henchard.

"You don't mind?"

"No, not at all. I will even give you money to live on. Then you will not be forced to live on the poor wages some wealthy employer would pay you. In fact, a small annuity is what I'd like you to have. Then you can be independent of me and I may be independent of you."

Elizabeth-Jane thanked Henchard and made plans to meet the young woman again.

The day came for their meeting, but it began to rain. Still, Elizabeth-Jane went to the churchyard as planned. The young woman came, too.

"Well," said the young woman, "have you decided?"

"Yes, quite."

"Your father is willing?"

"Yes."

"Then come along whenever you like. Can you come today?"

"I might be able to," said the girl.

"By the way, I have never told you my name. It is Miss Templeman."

Elizabeth-Jane hurried home to get her things

ready. Henchard was surprised when he came home and found her with her bags and boxes packed.

"But you said I could go, Father," she explained.

"Yes!" he replied. "But I thought you meant next month or next year. This, then, is how you are going to treat me for all my trouble?"

Henchard went up to her room to look around. Not all of her things had been brought down. He saw some books and pictures and pretty little things. He turned suddenly and came down to the door.

"Look here!" he said "Don't go away from me."

"Father," she said, "I think I had better go. I shall not be far away."

He nodded quietly. "Where will you be in case I wish to write to you?"

"I'll be in town, at High-Place Hall."

Mr. Henchard stood there with a surprised look on his face. He did not move or speak as she waved good-bye.

7 Lucetta Chooses

We must go back for a moment to the time before Elizabeth-Jane moved away. Then you will see why Henchard was so surprised.

Henchard had recently received a letter from Lucetta. She had told him that she knew Susan had died. She hoped Henchard would now marry her. The news pleased Henchard. He had felt very alone since learning that Elizabeth-Jane was not his child.

One night Henchard had gone to High-Place Hall to see Lucetta. (And Elizabeth-Jane had almost run into him.) He had asked if Lucetta was living there. He was told that only Miss Templeman did. Henchard decided that Lucetta had not yet moved in.

Before long Elizabeth-Jane had told Henchard where she would be living—at High-Place Hall. Suddenly it hit him! He remembered that Lucetta had often mentioned a rich relative named Templeman. He figured out that Lucetta and Miss Templeman must be the same person.

Now Henchard wanted very much to marry Lucetta. The thought that she might be rich made him very happy.

Lucetta's first meeting with Elizabeth-Jane had not

been planned. Yet Lucetta had quickly thought of a plan. If Elizabeth-Jane lived with her, Henchard would have a reason to visit. No one would have to know that Henchard and Lucetta had known each other in the past. So Lucetta invited the young girl into her home.

After Elizabeth had moved out, Henchard received another note from Lucetta. In it she explained that her relative had died and left her a large amount of money. That was when she'd decided to come to Casterbridge.

Henchard was happy about the way things were working out. He quickly went to visit Lucetta. But when he got there, he was told that she had gone out for the evening and would be happy to see him the next day.

The news bothered Henchard. "She is playing hard to get!" he thought. He knew that she had not expected him. Still, he decided not to visit her the next day.

In the meantime, Elizabeth-Jane had moved in. She was enjoying her new home. The two women seemed to like and trust each other.

Lucetta had promised herself that she would keep her past a secret. Nevertheless, she quickly told Elizabeth-Jane that she was from Jersey and not from Bath. Lucetta's secret was safe with Elizabeth-Jane. Her words went no further. The next morning, a Saturday, Lucetta got ready for Henchard's visit. She dressed herself carefully, hoping he would come in the morning. He did not come. She still waited through the afternoon.

The windows of High-Place Hall looked out over the town market. Every Saturday the businessmen and farmers met there to buy and sell. Henchard was so near, and yet he did not visit! He must have been too busy, Lucetta thought. He would come on Sunday or Monday. Lucetta dressed carefully every day, but Henchard did not come.

On Tuesday at breakfast, Lucetta said to Elizabeth-Jane, "I suppose your father will come to see you today."

Elizabeth-Jane shook her head. "He won't come."

"Why?"

"He has taken against me," she replied.

Lucetta was surprised at this. She began to think that her plan for having Henchard visit would not work. Now she would have to get rid of Elizabeth-Jane in some way.

After thinking a moment, Lucetta said, "Miss Henchard, will you go shopping for me when breakfast is over? Do take your time."

As soon as Elizabeth-Jane left, Lucetta sent a quick note to Henchard. She explained that Elizabeth-Jane would be out for a few hours and she asked Henchard to visit.

A short time later, she heard a man's step on the stairs to her sitting room. The door opened. But the man before her was not Henchard.

Lucetta blushed, and then she smiled.

The man was good-looking, well dressed, and years younger than the mayor of Casterbridge.

"I'm very sorry," the man said. "I came to see Miss Henchard, and the maid showed me up here. Is this the wrong house?"

"Oh no, sit down. Miss Henchard will be back soon."

That was not quite true. But something about the man made Lucetta wish for him to stay.

Donald Farfrae had come because of the note he received from Henchard. This was the note in which Henchard told Farfrae he could see Elizabeth-Jane. Farfrae was doing well in business, so he felt he was now able to marry. And who would make a better wife in every way than Elizabeth-Jane? Farfrae sat down to wait, and he and Lucetta got to know each other. He became so interested in Lucetta that he quite forgot that he had come to see Elizabeth-Jane.

Finally, Farfrae remembered he was supposed to meet someone at the market on business. He got up to leave and said, "I'll come another time—if I may?"

"Certainly," she said happily.

Farfrae left, with his mind full of thoughts of Lucetta. She watched him out the window as he walked through the market. A few minutes later, she heard a knock at the downstairs door. The maid came to tell her that it was the mayor.

"He's afraid he hasn't much time to spare," explained the maid.

"Oh! Then tell him I have a headache and won't see him today," said Lucetta.

When Elizabeth came home, Lucetta spoke to her in a kind voice. "I'm so glad you live here," she said. "You'll stay a long time, won't you?" Lucetta never said anything about Farfrae's visit.

Now Elizabeth's presence was a way to keep Henchard away—what a new idea! And it was a pleasing one to Lucetta. After all, Henchard had not paid attention to her.

After that, the two women lived for Saturdays. They might go out on other days, but both were sure to be home on Saturday. They sat at the window and watched the busy market with interest. They did not know they were both watching the same man.

One Saturday a new kind of farm machine was brought to the market. People were quite busy looking it over. Lucetta thought she and Elizabeth-Jane should see it, too. It was, after all, a good reason to visit the market.

Lucetta wore a bright red dress, a new one she had just bought. She and Elizabeth-Jane were carefully looking over the machine, when someone

said, "Good morning, Elizabeth-Jane."

Elizabeth-Jane looked up, and there was Henchard. Surprised, and not knowing what to do, she said, "This is the lady I live with, Father—Miss Templeman."

Henchard put his hand to his hat. Miss Templeman bowed.

"I am happy to meet you, Mr. Henchard," said Lucetta. They began to discuss the machine.

Henchard then said something very odd. Elizabeth-Jane wondered if she had heard him correctly. He said, "You refused to see me!" He seemed to be speaking to Lucetta.

Lucetta was ignoring him. Both women had suddenly forgotten about Henchard. They heard someone humming a Scottish song. It was Farfrae! He had come to see the machine. Before long he and the two women were talking together. Somehow, Elizabeth-Jane felt that she was in the way.

Later Lucetta explained to Elizabeth how she had known Donald when they saw him in the market. "I happened to meet Mr. Farfrae the other day, and so I knew him this morning," she said.

Elizabeth-Jane began to pay closer attention to Lucetta. A few days later, she watched Lucetta get ready to go out. Elizabeth-Jane knew Lucetta was hoping to see Farfrae.

When Lucetta came home, Elizabeth asked, "You've seen Mr. Farfrae today?"

"Yes," said Lucetta. "How did you know?" She did not tell Elizabeth-Jane how she had seen him.

The next morning Lucetta told Elizabeth-Jane that she had something on her mind. It was something about another person, a friend of hers.

"Suppose a lady once loved a man very much," said Lucetta. "He did not love her as well; but out of kindness, he promised to marry her. Then something happened, and they could not marry. The woman was very sad. Then things changed, and he wanted to marry her. In the meantime, my friend had met a man she liked better. Now comes the point: could she refuse to marry the first?"

"I can't answer," said Elizabeth-Jane thoughtfully. "It is so difficult."

Later Elizabeth-Jane thought about Lucetta's story. She knew that the "she" of the story was Lucetta herself.

Soon Farfrae began to visit High-Place Hall. He was kind and acted as if he was to be visiting both women. But in fact, Elizabeth-Jane felt left out. Donald appeared not to see her at all. He looked only at Lucetta. Elizabeth-Jane always found a reason to leave the room during such visits. Watching them together was too painful for her.

As the days passed and Henchard did not hear from Lucetta, he gave in and visited her again. Elizabeth-Jane was not at home. Lucetta seemed very distant.

"I have come to say that I am ready to marry you," Henchard said. "You set the day or month. You know more about these things than I."

"It is early yet," she said.

"Yes, I suppose it is. Still, I feel I owe it to you to marry as soon as possible. Well, what do you say?"

"For the time being, let things be," she answered.

"That's the way the wind blows, is it?" Henchard asked at last. Then he left.

8 Henchard's Fall

Henchard began to see that Donald Farfrae and Lucetta were in love. The angry Henchard decided to hire Joshua Jopp as his manager. After all, he had almost hired him once—before Farfrae had come along.

Henchard said to Jopp, "Now, one thing is important to me. The Scotchman, who is doing so well in business, must be cut out. We two can't live side by side—that's certain."

"I've seen it all," said Jopp.

"We must be fair, of course," Henchard said. "But hard, too. We will grind him into the ground—starve him out. I've the money, and I can do it."

Jopp agreed.

Henchard had a plan to put Farfrae out of business. He went to see a weather forecaster. The forecaster told Henchard to expect a bad harvest. Henchard knew a bad harvest would double the price of grain. So he bought all the grain he could and stored it away to sell later.

All through June the weather was bad. In July, however, the weather changed. The dull gray sky cleared to a bright blue. Everyone except Henchard was happy. A blue sky meant a good harvest.

Henchard was furious with himself. Why had he believed the weather forecaster? Now he would have to sell his grain at a loss. To make matters worse, he had bought on credit. To pay back his loans, he had to give most of his property to the Casterbridge Bank.

One day, while coming down the steps of the bank, Henchard saw Jopp. Jopp was taking off his hat to wipe his forehead. He said to a passing friend, "A fine hot day."

"Just wipe and say it's a fine hot day!" cried Henchard angrily. "Why did you let me buy?" Then he went on yelling until he ended up firing Jopp.

"You shall be sorry for this, sir!" said Jopp, as Henchard walked away.

Meanwhile, Donald Farfrae bought the cheap grain and grew richer.

One evening Henchard decided he would try to see Lucetta again. He knocked at her door, but the maid said that Lucetta was going out for the evening. Henchard walked away and stood on the other side of the street. He waited in the shadows and watched Lucetta's door.

In a moment Farfrae went to the door and knocked. Lucetta must have been waiting for him. She opened the door herself. As they walked off together, Henchard decided to follow.

The two walked out into the country, not noticing Henchard. When they stopped, Henchard came close enough to hear them talk. It was clear they were in love. Henchard listened a little while and then left. Later he returned to Lucetta's house and walked straight up to her sitting room.

Lucetta soon appeared. When she saw Henchard, she let out a frightened little cry. "You have no right to surprise me here!" she said.

"You are wrong, Lucetta," Henchard replied. He reminded Lucetta of their past together and asked her to marry him. When she refused, Henchard became angry.

"You cannot refuse me," he said. "Promise—before a witness—that you will marry me, or I will reveal your past."

A look of bitterness came over Lucetta's face. She sent her maid to get Elizabeth-Jane.

When Elizabeth-Jane entered the room, Henchard took her hand and said, "I want you to hear this." Then he turned to Lucetta and said, "Will you, or will you not, marry me?"

"If you wish it, I must agree!" she exclaimed.

"You say yes?"

"I do," she answered and fainted.

Elizabeth knelt down by Lucetta. "What drives her to say this?" she asked. "It is clearly very painful to her, Father. Please don't make her do this."

"Don't be foolish," said Henchard. "This promise will leave Donald free for you if you want him."

Lucetta awoke, and Henchard left.

Elizabeth said, "I'll go ask him to set you free."

"No, no," said Lucetta. "Let it all be."

The next morning Henchard went to the town hall to attend court. He was a judge in the town court. That day, an old woman in faded clothes and a sticky black bonnet stood before the court. She was charged with disorderly conduct and with making a mess on a church wall.

After hearing the charges, Henchard turned to the woman. "Now then, what can you say for yourself?" he asked.

She replied, "Twenty years ago I was selling furmity in a tent at Weydon Fair. . ."

Henchard stared at her, forgetting all about the charges. The woman went on to tell how Henchard had sold his wife and child.

Everybody in the courtroom looked at Henchard. His face looked pale and strange.

"We don't want to hear your lies," said the clerk. "What can you say about the case?"

"This *is* about the case," the woman said. "It proves that he's not any better than I am. He has no right to judge me."

The next words came from Henchard. "It's true,"

he said slowly. "It's as true as light. And it does prove that I'm no better than she!"

Henchard left the chair and went outside. The story of what happened spread quickly through the town. When she heard the story from her maid, Lucetta was shocked. How terrible it would be to marry such a man!

Later that day, Lucetta told Elizabeth-Jane that she was going away to Port Bredy for a few days. Elizabeth-Jane saw her off, then took charge of High-Place Hall until her return.

A few days later, Henchard called at the house. "She returned this morning," Elizabeth-Jane told him. "But she has gone for a walk along the road to Port Bredy." With that, Henchard left, disappointed.

Elizabeth-Jane then decided to go out and meet Lucetta along the road. As they walked together, they saw an escaped bull in the fields. It was shaking its head and coming their way. The two women ran inside a nearby barn. The bull charged in after them.

They raced from one end of the barn to the other, with the bull following. He was so close that they could feel the breath from his nostrils. No one can say what might have happened if a man had not suddenly come in to save them.

The man grabbed the bull by the horns. Then he led it to the door. At last, the two women saw that it was Henchard. He tied the bull outside, then quickly went to help Lucetta, who was terribly frightened.

Henchard began walking the two women home, but Elizabeth-Jane remembered she had dropped a glove in the barn. She went back for it. Henchard and Lucetta walked on. Just then Elizabeth-Jane saw a carriage coming. Donald Farfrae was in it. Now she knew why Lucetta had gone for a walk.

Donald saw Elizabeth-Jane and stopped. She quickly told him what had happened. He appeared worried. "She has gone on with Mr. Henchard, you say?" he asked at last.

"Yes. He is taking her home."

"Your stepfather saved her?" Donald asked,

amazed. Then he drove Elizabeth-Jane into town.

While Farfrae and Elizabeth-Jane were talking, Henchard and Lucetta were talking as well. Henchard took Lucetta's hand.

"Dear Lucetta," he said. "I have been thinking about the way I got your promise that night. I don't want to make you unhappy. So we can put off our marriage for a year or two."

Then Lucetta told Henchard her news. "Donald Farfrae and I were married this week at Port Bredy. We didn't want to marry here."

Henchard stood as if he had turned to stone.

"I loved him so much," Lucetta said with tears in her eyes, "And then I heard how you had sold your first wife like a horse! How could I marry you after hearing that? You will not tell Donald about my past, will you, Michael? It is too late to separate us."

"Oh, you false woman!" cried Henchard. "I should punish you and tell your new husband about us."

"Michael, pity me!"

"You don't deserve pity!"

"I'll help you pay off your debts," she cried.

"Never. Now go home."

Lucetta drank some ale in an effort to calm herself before Donald got home. When he arrived, she met him with great joy.

"Now there is one more thing to do," she said. "I must tell my dear Elizabeth-Jane that we are married. I'll go to her now. And Donald, you don't mind her living here, do you?" she asked.

"Oh, no, I don't," answered Farfrae. "But I wonder if she will want to?"

"I am sure she will!" said Lucetta. "Besides, the poor girl has no other home."

Lucetta went to Elizabeth-Jane's room. Just then, wedding bells began to ring.

"Hello, Miss Templeman," Elizabeth-Jane said. "I went downstairs to see you, but you had a visitor. I wonder why the bells are ringing?"

"Well, now, I have something to tell you." Lucetta paused. "Do you remember my story about the old lover and the new lover?"

Elizabeth-Jane remembered. "I recall that you—or your friend—decided to do the wrong thing."

"But Elizabeth-Jane," Lucetta said. "the first man turned out to be a terrible man."

Right and wrong were very clear to Elizabeth-Jane. She said, "You must marry the first man—or remain a single woman."

Lucetta covered her eyes with her right hand. She held out her left to Elizabeth-Jane.

"Why, you have married him!" cried Elizabeth-Jane happily.

"Oh, my Elizabeth-Jane!" cried Lucetta. "I have married someone else."

"You . . . have married Mr. Farfrae!" cried

Elizabeth-Jane, with tears in her eyes.

Lucetta nodded. "My husband is downstairs. We will live here until we find another house. But I want you to stay with me just as before."

"Let me think about it," the girl replied, trying to control her feelings.

"I am sure we shall be happy together," said Lucetta as she left the room.

Elizabeth-Jane knew she could not live in that house. She quickly went out and found a new place to live. She packed up her things, wrote a note for Lucetta, and moved out of High-Place Hall.

Elizabeth's new home was on Corn Street, almost directly across the street from Henchard's. She sat down and began to think about how to make a living. Meanwhile, the rest of the town discussed young Farfrae's marriage.

9 Losses

Once everyone in Casterbridge knew the furmity woman's story, Henchard's recent good deeds were quickly forgotten. It was strange how easily Henchard lost the people's respect.

Henchard's hard luck seemed to know no end. Soon his fortunes began to decrease. A person who owed him money could not pay. Then one of his workers sold bad wheat. It ruined Henchard's name. Soon the town bankers and farmers met with Henchard. He had to sell everything he owned.

Henchard looked very pale. "Gentlemen," he said, "I don't wish to keep anything from you."

He laid his gold watch on the table. He also untied his moneybag and shook the contents out. He leaned over to take back a small gift Lucetta had once given him.

"There," he said. "Now you have all I've got in the world. I wish for your sakes that it were more."

The bankers looked at the watch. Farmer Everdene spoke.

"No, no, Henchard," he said. "You keep that."

The others agreed. "You have behaved rashly," said the top banker. "But you have been fair. You did not mean to do anything wrong. That is clear."

Out on the streets, Henchard scolded himself. "I have no right to this watch," he said. "Why didn't they take it?"

He took the watch to the watchmaker's and sold it on the spot. Then he took the money to a poor man whom he had once borrowed from.

When the auction of Henchard's goods began, people began to feel sorry for him. After all, he had come to town with nothing but energy, and he had made a fortune. They were sorry he had lost it all.

Elizabeth-Jane was tearful when she found out. She wrote to him, but he did not reply. Then she went to his house—the great house in which she had lived so happily. But he was not there. He had sold his lovely home. Now he rented a room in Jopp's cottage. Elizabeth-Jane went there, but Henchard could not be seen.

"Not by his daughter?" Elizabeth-Jane begged.

"By nobody; that's his order," she was told.

Elizabeth-Jane passed by Henchard's former business on her way home. Farfrae's name was now painted on the gate.

Henchard soon began to visit a lonely bridge on the outskirts of town. Over the years, many unhappy men had stood there and stared down into the water. The powerless had wished they were kings. The poor had wished they were rich. And the lonely had wished for love. Some of the men had stopped staring into the water and jumped in.

Henchard was at the foot of the bridge when Jopp came by and told him some news. "He and she are in their new house today," he said. "Your house."

"My house? They moved into my house?" cried Henchard.

"And Farfrae bought all your best furniture at the auction," Jopp went on.

"My furniture too! Surely he'll buy my body and soul as well," replied Henchard.

Henchard walked onto the bridge. The lands around looked blacker, the sky a deeper gray. He stared fixedly into the racing river below. As he stood there, a carriage drove by. A voice called to him.

"Mr Henchard? I have heard that you are thinking of leaving Casterbridge. Is it true?"

Henchard looked up. It was Farfrae. "Yes," he replied. "I can't stay here and do nothing."

Farfrae offered Henchard some rooms in the house that had once been Henchard's. Henchard thought about being in the same house with Donald and Lucetta.

"No!" he answered. "You don't know what you're asking. But I must thank you for the offer."

"By the by," said Farfrae. "I bought a bit of your furniture."

"So I heard," said Henchard.

"Well, I wish you to pick out all that you like. You might need some things, and I can always get more."

"What!" exclaimed Henchard. "You would just give it to me?" Henchard looked troubled. "Farfrae, sometimes I think I wronged you."

Meanwhile, Elizabeth-Jane was living quietly in her tiny room across the street from Henchard's old house. The Farfraes now lived there. She could see Donald and Lucetta happily coming and going. She tried to keep from watching them, but she was only human. She couldn't help looking up when she heard the doors slam.

One day Elizabeth-Jane heard the news that Henchard was sick. She went off to Jopp's cottage at once. This time she was determined to see him. She went directly in.

"Go away—go away," he said when he saw her. "I don't like to see you."

Elizabeth-Jane cared for Henchard until he was well. She quickly became his friend.

When he was well again, Henchard went to Farfrae's place of business and asked for a job cutting hay. He was hired at once. For a while things went well. At the beginning of winter, however, Henchard learned that Farfrae was going to be mayor.

Henchard became moody. He began to hate the

Scotchman. He also began to talk about his old promise not to drink.

"In twelve days I shall be free of my oath," he told a workman. "And then I mean to enjoy myself!"

One Sunday, Elizabeth-Jane overheard some people talking below her window. "Michael Henchard has busted out drinking!" someone said.

Elizabeth-Jane jumped up and went out to look for Henchard. He had chosen the Three Mariners Inn as the place to take his first strong drink. The place was full of townspeople.

"How are you, Mr. Henchard?" The customers nodded to him.

Henchard quickly began drinking. Then he saw Farfrae and Lucetta pass by on their way home from church. He began making threats about Farfrae.

"I could double him up like this," he said. And he took an iron poker and bent it across his knee. It was just then that Elizabeth-Jane entered the place. She took Henchard by the arm and begged him to go home.

Henchard drank at the Three Mariners every evening after that. Elizabeth-Jane tried to keep him from drinking strong liquor. She carried tea to him in a little basket each evening. It did no good, of course. Henchard kept his dark thoughts.

Finally, Elizabeth-Jane decided that she had to warn Donald about Henchard. One morning she arose at five o'clock to wait for Farfrae outside. It was not yet light. There was a thick fog, and the town was as silent as it was dark. Farfrae was walking toward his business when he saw her.

"What . . . Miss Henchard! Are you up so early?"

"I have something important to tell you," she said.

"Yes?" he said. "And what may it be?"

Elizabeth-Jane explained her fears.

"But we are quite friendly," answered Farfrae. He told her she worried for nothing, and they parted. Elizabeth-Jane was very unhappy. She felt like a fool.

Farfrae did not forget Elizabeth-Jane's warning. He knew she was a solid young woman, and he trusted her judgment. Still, he decided to go on helping Henchard. He wanted to give Henchard a start in a small seed business. He would put up half the money if the town council would put up the rest. He took his plan to the town clerk.

"About that little seed shop," Farfrae said. "It would be a new beginning for Henchard."

"Yes, yes," the town clerk replied. "But Farfrae, others see what you do not. Henchard hates you, and it's right that you should know it. He was at the Three Mariners last night saying terrible things about you."

"Is that so?" said Farfrae, looking down. "Why should he do it?" he added bitterly. "What harm have I done him that he should try to wrong me?"

Farfrae told the town clerk he would not fire

Henchard. "But I'll drop the plan for the seed shop until I can think more about it."

Later, the owner of the seed shop told Henchard that his shop was for sale. He said the town council wanted to buy the shop for Henchard. He blamed Donald Farfrae for holding up the sale. Henchard's hatred of Farfrae grew stronger still.

In the meantime, Lucetta became more and more worried that Henchard would tell Donald about her past. When Donald came home she spoke to him.

"Give up the business, and let's go away from here," she begged him. "We have plenty of money, and why should we stay?"

Donald had been ready to discuss leaving, when someone came to the door with a message. The mayor, Dr. Chalkfields, had died suddenly. Would Donald agree to be the next mayor?

"We were thinking of going away," said Lucetta weakly.

"It was only a fancy," Farfrae murmured. "If I am needed, I must not refuse."

When the man had gone, Farfrae told Lucetta, "See how we are ruled by the Powers above us! We plan this, but we do that. If they want me to be mayor, then I will stay. Henchard must rave as he will."

When Henchard heard that Farfrae was the new mayor, he almost told him about Lucetta's past. But he stopped short. Such a wrecking of hearts was too mean even for him.

Lucetta continued to worry. She sent Henchard a note, asking him to meet her at the Ring. She dressed carefully for the meeting. She went without sleep so that the worry would show on her face. She wore her poorest, plainest, and oldest dress. Then she walked to the Ring, taking care that no one would see her.

Henchard met her there, in the same place he had once met Susan. He saw how worn she looked. It made him think of Susan, the other poor woman who had suffered because of him. Henchard's anger faded at once. He decided that such a woman was a very small deer to hunt. Suddenly he felt ashamed.

"Well, what do you want me to do?" he asked gently.

"Give me back the letters and any papers that say anything about our marriage—or worse."

"So be it. Every scrap shall be yours. And don't doubt me. I can keep my word. But Lucetta," he added, "Donald is sure to find out sooner or later."

"Ah!" she said. "But not until I have proven I am a good and faithful wife! Then maybe he will forgive my past."

That night Henchard packaged up the letters and went to Jopp.

"I wish you would do me a favor, Jopp," he said.

"Please take this to Mrs. Farfrae. I would do it myself, but I don't wish to be seen there."

He handed Jopp a sealed package wrapped in brown paper. Jopp agreed to deliver the package, but he became curious. He had guessed there was something between Lucetta and Henchard. Now he had a package from one to the other.

Jopp carefully lifted the wax seal of the package and looked inside. He saw that it was a bundle of letters. Satisfied, he sealed the package again and went off to deliver it.

On his way, Jopp ran into his friends Mrs. Cuxsom and Nance Mockridge.

"We are going down to Mixen Lane," said Mrs. Cuxsom. "There's fiddle music going on at Peter's Finger. Do come along, too, Jopp."

Jopp decided to stop at the inn with the two women. At first glance, Peter's Finger looked quite respectable. The steps were clean, the door was shut, and no one was standing—or lying—outside. However, it was not rare for someone to walk along the street near the inn and suddenly disappear. This was because its real entrance was in the alley. People would stroll down the street, then edge into the alley. Once in the alley, they would slip in the door.

Peter's Finger was a place of petty thieves and vagrants. The worst people at the Three Mariners

knew the best people at Peter's. The old furmity woman was among Peter's customers. She was the one who asked Jopp about his package.

"Ah, that's a grand secret," said Jopp. "They are love letters."

"Love letters? Then let's hear them," said Mrs. Cuxsom. "Lord! Do you remember what fools we used to be?"

By this time, Jopp had unsealed the package. He began reading the letters aloud. Of course, this uncovered Lucetta's buried secret.

"Mrs. Farfrae wrote that?" asked Nance Mockridge. "What a shameful woman. I say! What a good reason for a skimmity ride."

"What is a skimmity ride?" someone asked.

"Oh, it's an old foolish thing they do here when a man's wife is untrue," said the innkeeper.

The innkeeper went on to explain that people held a parade to make fun of the married couple. Some people found it funny, but she thought it cruel.

In any case, Jopp's group made plans for the skimmity ride. Then Jopp gathered up the letters and sealed the package again. Since it was late, he delivered them to Lucetta the next morning. Within an hour, Lucetta had burned all the letters. The poor soul believed her secret was finally safe.

10 Some Shameful Acts

That was the way things stood when the town of Casterbridge learned some exciting and important news. . . . a member of the royal family would be passing through town! It was a great honor, and the whole town was thrilled. The town council decided to do something special in honor of the visit.

The council members met on Tuesday to make plans. Henchard came in while they were meeting. He was wearing the same suit he had worn when he was mayor. Now it was old and shabby.

"I have the feeling," Henchard said, "that I would like to join you in meeting the royal guest. I suppose I could walk with the rest?"

Everyone looked away, not wanting to answer.

Finally, Farfrae answered, "I don't think it would be proper, Mr. Henchard. You are no longer one of the council. If we included you, why not others? I think everyone here feels that way." He looked around.

"Yes, yes," answered Doctor Bath and Lawyer Long.

Henchard angrily turned around and left.

When the big day arrived, Henchard did not go to work. He started the day with a strong drink. Then he went to the center of town, where people were waiting for the royal visitor.

The royal carriage arrived, stopping in front of the Town Hall. Before anyone could stop him, Henchard stumbled up to the carriage waving a flag. He held his hand out to the royal guest. Mayor Farfrae quickly grabbed Henchard, pushed him back into the crowd, and roughly told him to leave. Then Farfrae made his own address to the royal visitor. He and Lucetta both shook hands with the royalty.

Henchard was still angry when he met Jopp later that afternoon. As a rival, Farfrae had beat Henchard. As a boss, he had snubbed his former patron. Now Farfrae was shaking him by the collar like a common vagrant.

Henchard muttered to himself, "He drove me back like a bull breaking a fence. I took it like a lamb. But he shall pay for it. It must come to a fight—face to face."

Henchard then went to Farfrae's house and left a message for Farfrae to meet him at the grain barn. Henchard returned to a shed, took a short piece of rope, and tightly tied his left arm against his body. Then he went up the ladder to the top floor of the barn. He opened the upper barn door and looked down. It was 30 or 40 feet to the ground below.

When Farfrae arrived, Henchard called out, "Will you come up here?"

"Yes," said Farfrae, as he climbed slowly up. "What's wrong?"

Henchard said quietly, "Now we stand face to face—man to man. We'll finish what you began this morning."

"There's the door, 40 feet above the ground," Henchard continued. "One of us shoves the other out that door. The other stays inside. If he likes, the winner can say the other fell out by accident. Or he can tell the truth. I am the stronger man, so I have tied one arm to be fair."

There was no time for Farfrae to do anything but fight. But the Scotchman was a small man. Even though he used only one arm, Henchard was still able to defeat Farfrae. Henchard had him on the floor. Farfrae was halfway out the door, head first.

"Now," said Henchard, "your life is in my hands."

"Then take it!" cried Farfrae. "You've wished for it long enough!"

Henchard looked down at him, and their eyes met. "Oh, Farfrae!" he cried. "That is not true! I loved you as a friend. And now . . . though I came to kill you, I cannot."

Henchard turned Farfrae loose and stepped back. Farfrae left without saying a word.

Henchard sat there in the barn, thinking about the shameful thing he had just done. He remembered the first time he had met Farfrae.

"He thought highly of me once," thought Henchard. "Now he'll hate me forever."

He turned to leave as Farfrae sat talking to one of the workers. Farfrae was explaining that he would not be going to Budmouth but to Weatherbury instead.

After Farfrae's carriage left, Henchard walked to the old stone bridge. As he stood looking at the water, he heard loud noises coming from town. He did not pay any attention—he was still thinking of his shame.

Later that day, Lucetta sat in her room waiting for Farfrae to come home. She was happy. She was thinking about the day and about meeting and shaking hands with the royal visitor. Then she began to hear noises in the distance, the noises were coming closer and closer. Outside, she heard women calling to one another.

"Which way are they going now?" said one.

"They are coming up Corn Street," was the answer. "I can see two figures on a donkey, back to back. She's facing the head, and he's facing the tail."

"Who is it supposed to be?"

"Well, one is dressed just as she was dressed when she met the royalty today!"

Lucetta jumped up. At the same moment, the door opened and Elizabeth-Jane stepped in.

"I have come to see you," she said, out of breath.

"I . . . I see your windows are open. Let me close them for you."

Lucetta stopped her. "It's me!" she said, her face pale as death. "They are making fun of him and me."

"Let me close the window," said Elizabeth-Jane softly.

"It's no use!" she screamed. "He will see it, won't he? Donald will see it. He will never love me anymore—and it will kill me—kill me!" Lucetta fell to the floor in a faint.

Elizabeth-Jane called for a doctor.

As soon as the doctor saw Lucetta, he said, "This is serious. Send for Mr. Farfrae at once."

Soon a man was riding off toward Budmouth, where everyone believed Farfrae had gone.

Long before this time, Henchard had gone into town. He had seen the figures in the skimmity ride, and he knew what they meant. He went looking for Elizabeth-Jane. He was told she was at Farfrae's house, so he went there. A group of men were leaving to help find Farfrae in Budmouth.

"But Farfrae has gone to Weatherbury, not Budmouth," Henchard said. No one believed him, however.

Henchard, ashamed and sorry for what he had done, decided to find Farfrae himself. He ran off on foot out of town.

When he finally found Farfrae, Henchard called, "Come back to Casterbridge at once! There's something wrong at your house. You must come back!"

Farfrae stopped his carriage for a moment and looked at Henchard in silence. Henchard knew that Farfrae didn't believe him.

"I have to go to Mellstock," Farfrae said coldly.

"But the matter is more serious than your business there," Henchard said. "It is your wife, she is ill. Oh, Farfrae, don't mistrust me. I am a wretchful man, but my heart is true to you still."

But Farfrae did distrust him—completely. He drove off, leaving Henchard to walk back to Casterbridge.

When he reached the Farfrae home, Henchard knocked and entered. He found Elizabeth-Jane there.

"How is she?" he asked.

"Poor woman. I fear they have killed her!" answered Elizabeth-Jane.

Henchard left for his cottage, thinking about Elizabeth-Jane. She seemed like a ray of light in the midst of all the sadness.

About two hours later, Farfrae finally returned home. He was upset to learn that Henchard had been telling the truth. His wife was very ill. He sat with her through the night. During this time, Lucetta told Donald about her past. No one knows exactly what she said to him.

Henchard, still upset, could not sleep. He spent the night walking up and down Corn Street in front of the Farfrae's home. Every once in a while, he would knock and ask about Lucetta.

Just at dawn, a maid stepped out of the door. She removed a piece of cloth that had been wrapped around the door knocker.

"Why do you take that off?" asked Henchard.

The woman turned, surprised to see him. "Because people may knock as loud as they wish. She will never hear it anymore."

11 A New Beginning

Henchard went home. Soon afterward, Elizabeth-Jane came knocking at his door. Henchard's face brightened when he saw her.

"Mrs. Farfrae is dead," she said.

"I know," he answered. "But it's good of you to come. You must be tired after sitting up all night."

He told her to take a nap and he would cook her breakfast. She lay down on a couch in the next room and was soon asleep.

Henchard fixed breakfast for Elizabeth-Jane and kept it warm while she slept. In truth, his feelings about her had changed. He was beginning to think of her again as his daughter.

Suddenly, Henchard heard another knock at the door. When he opened it, he saw a strongly built man before him. It was no one he knew.

"Good morning," said the stranger in a friendly way. "Mr. Henchard?"

"My name is Henchard."

"Good. May I have a few words with you?"

Henchard invited him in.

"You may remember me," said the stranger. "My name is Newson. We met a long time ago."

Henchard's face and eyes seemed to die. "I know the name well," he said at last, looking at the floor.

Newson went on to tell his story. He told how Henchard's baby had died. Newson and Susan had another baby, whom they named Elizabeth-Jane. The family lived happily together for a time.

Susan became unhappy with Newson upon finding out the sale was not a legal marriage. Newson formed a plan to give her freedom. He let Susan believe that he was dead when his ship was once lost in a storm. He thought it was the kindest thing to do. He believed that Susan would then go back to Henchard.

"They told me in Falmouth that Susan was dead. But my Elizabeth-Jane, where is she?"

"Dead also," said Henchard quietly. "Surely you heard that, too?"

The sailor jumped up. "Dead!" he said in a low voice. "Then what's the use of my money to me? When did she die?"

"A year ago and more," replied Henchard quickly.

"My trip here has been for nothing. I may as well go. I'll bother you no longer." With that, Newson left.

Henchard was amazed at himself. The words had just come out of his mouth. He had not thought at all. His loneliness and his new love for Elizabeth-Jane had caused him to lie.

Henchard began to worry that Newson would ask around town and find out the truth. He quickly put on his hat. He decided he would follow Newson and tell him the truth. But Newson was already riding off in a carriage when Henchard caught sight of him. Newson had trusted him. Henchard stood there, ashamed.

Before long Henchard returned home to find Elizabeth-Jane just waking. He didn't tell her about Newson. But he worried that Newson would return someday. Elizabeth-Jane would find out the truth, and she would no longer call him Father.

A year passed. Donald Farfrae found that time

helped him get over Lucetta. Her death had caused him much sorrow, but their life together might have been a constant misery. He could not believe that they would have been happy after the scandal they had suffered.

Henchard swallowed his pride and accepted money to start a small seed business. He and Elizabeth-Jane settled in town. They got along well. Henchard's business grew, and Henchard seemed content.

Elizabeth-Jane started taking long walks in the country. Henchard noticed that she had many books and was often buying new clothes. One day at the marketplace, Henchard saw Farfrae staring at something. Turning to look, Henchard saw that Farfrae was staring at Elizabeth-Jane.

Henchard did not think that a marriage between Farfrae and Elizabeth-Jane would be good for both the girl and himself. He hated the thought of it. He feared that he was losing his stepdaughter.

Henchard began to watch Elizabeth-Jane more closely. He even followed her on her walks down Budmouth Road. That's where he saw her meet Farfrae.

"He means to rob me of her, too!" he whispered to himself. "But he has the right. I won't try to stop them."

One day Henchard saw another man walking

along the road. At first, he thought it was Farfrae. But then he saw the man's face. Henchard aged a lifetime the moment he saw it. The face was Newson's.

When Henchard returned home, Elizabeth-Jane said, "Father, I have received an unsigned letter. Someone has asked me to meet him tonight at Mr. Farfrae's. He said that he had come to see me some time ago but that someone had played a trick on him. Shall I go?"

Henchard replied heavily, "Yes, go."

Then he surprised her by saying, "I am going to leave Casterbridge, Elizabeth-Jane. You can manage the shop alone."

She looked down, and her tears fell silently. She thought he was leaving because she was seeing Farfrae. But she loved Farfrae, so she said, "I am sorry you have decided this. I thought I might marry Mr. Farfrae soon. I didn't know you were so against it."

"I approve of anything you want to do, Izzy," said Henchard. "But I must go. Think of me sometimes, will you? No matter what you hear about me. And don't forget that although I loved you late, I loved you well."

"I won't forget," she promised.

That evening Elizabeth-Jane went to Farfrae's for her meeting. Farfrae opened the door to the sitting room for her and he said, "There he is, waiting for you."

It was Richard Newson. The meeting was a wonderfully happy one. Elizabeth-Jane still loved the man who had raised her. And Newson was very proud of how his daughter had grown up. They sat and talked, and Farfrae invited Newson to stay for the wedding.

Newson then told the story of his earlier visit to Casterbridge. He laughed about it, thinking it was a good joke. But Elizabeth-Jane was shocked.

"A joke? He kept you from me, Father, all those months. I said I would never forget him, but I wish I could forget him now!"

That night Henchard left Casterbridge secretly. "I go alone, as I deserve. But my punishment is not greater than I can bear!" he said to himself.

12 Henchard's Unhappy End

Henchard walked until he was too tired to go on. Then he lay down in a field and slept. When morning came he ate the food he had packed before he left.

Henchard walked for days. On the afternoon of the sixth day, he reached Weydon-Priors—the place where his unhappy story had begun. He had not planned to stay, but he was thinking of Elizabeth-Jane. He could still get news about her here.

Henchard found work cutting hay, just as he had done long ago. Often he stopped working and looked off in the direction of Casterbridge. He wondered what Elizabeth-Jane was doing at those moments. He eagerly stopped to talk to people passing along the road. He hoped for news from Casterbridge. That was how he learned the day of Elizabeth-Jane's marriage to Farfrae.

What if he had been wrong about Newson, he wondered. What if Newson had not returned or Elizabeth-Jane had not welcomed him? Maybe there had been no reason for him to leave! Henchard decided to go to the wedding.

He began walking two days before the wedding. Since he had no good clothes, he stopped at a town along the way to buy some. Then he decided to buy Elizabeth-Jane a present.

Henchard walked up and down the street, looking in shop windows. At last he decided on a songbird, a beautiful goldfinch in a cage. The cage was small and plain, so he could afford it. He wrapped up the gift in newspaper, then found a place to stay.

The next day he set out walking again. At last he could hear the Casterbridge church bells ringing. It was a sure sign that the wedding had taken place. Since it was only noon, Henchard waited outside of town until dark. He dusted his boots and washed his hands at the river. Then he went to Farfrae's house.

Henchard saw the house all lit up. The doors were open, and people were coming and going. He almost turned back, afraid he would not be welcome. Then he went around back to the kitchen door. He set the bird and cage under a bush outside and knocked on the door.

The maid let him in and told him to wait. Henchard could see the dancers through the partly opened door. He caught sight of Elizabeth-Jane in a snowy white dress, with a look of pleasure on her face. Then Henchard saw the face of her dancing partner. It was Newson.

He would have left, but the dance ended just then. Elizabeth-Jane walked into the room.

"Oh! It is . . . Mr. Henchard!" she said coldly.

"Elizabeth!" he cried and took her hand. "You call me Mr. Henchard? Don't hurt me like that! Call me worthless old Henchard! Call me anything—but don't be so cold as this!"

He went on, "I see you have another—real—father in my place. Then you know everything. But do save a little room for me!"

Elizabeth pulled her hand away gently. "I could have loved you always. But how can I after you have lied to me? How can I love a man who has treated me like that!"

Henchard started to say something to explain. But he closed his lips and didn't answer. How could he give any excuse for what he had done?

"Don't upset yourself because of me," he said proudly. "It was wrong of me to come here. I'll never bother you again. Not to my dying day! Good-bye!"

Henchard left the house before Elizabeth-Jane had time to think. He went out the back way, as he had come in. She saw no more of him.

A week after the wedding, Elizabeth-Jane found a bird cage in the garden. At the bottom was a little ball of feathers—the dead body of a goldfinch. It was clear that the little songbird had starved to death. The sadness of it bothered Elizabeth-Jane for days.

Then her maid told Elizabeth-Jane what had happened. "It was that man who came the evening of the wedding. I saw him come up the street with it in his hand. He must have forgotten it."

Elizabeth-Jane decided Henchard must have brought the bird as a wedding gift. She went out to bury the little dead bird. Her heart soon softened toward Henchard.

When her husband came in, Elizabeth-Jane told him about the bird. Then she begged Donald to help her find Henchard. She wanted to tell him she was sorry and to help him if she could.

Farfrae asked around and found out in which direction Henchard had gone. The next morning he and Elizabeth-Jane set out to find him. They stopped at Egdon, but Henchard had not been there. Farfrae drove on, but it seemed that Henchard had sunk into the earth.

It was getting late. They were about to turn when they saw someone cross the road and go into a small cottage.

"If we were in Casterbridge, I would say that was Abel Whittle," said Elizabeth-Jane. "It looks just like him."

"It might be Whittle," answered Donald. "He's been gone for three weeks—no one knows where."

They stopped and walked up to the cottage. The walls of the cottage were crumbling, held together only by climbing ivy. The roof was full of holes. Farfrae knocked on the door, and Whittle answered.

His face showed a deep sadness.

"Abel Whittle, is that you?" said Farfrae.

"Yes, sir! You see, he was kind to mother when she was still alive, though he was rough to me."

"Who are you talking about?"

"Oh, sir, Mr. Henchard! Didn't you know? He's just gone—about half an hour ago."

"Dead?" cried Elizabeth-Jane.

"Yes, ma'am, he's gone! He was kind to mother when she was alive. He sent her his best coal and other things she needed. I saw him go down the street the night of your wedding. I thought he looked low, so I followed. He turned and saw me and said 'You go back!' But I followed. I saw he was low.

"We walked on like that all night. I saw he could hardly drag along. By that time, we had got here. I saw the house was empty, so I helped him inside. Some neighbors lent me a bed and a chair. We made him comfortable as we could. But he was weak. He couldn't eat. He kept getting weaker, and today he died."

"Dear me," said Farfrae. Elizabeth-Jane said nothing.

"He pinned a piece of paper to the headboard," said Abel Whittle. "I can't read writing, so I don't know what it is. I can get it and show you."

The man brought out the scrap of paper. These words were written on it:

Michael Henchard's Will

That Elizabeth-Jane Farfrae not be told of my
death or made to grieve because of me,
& that I not be buried in church ground,
& that no minister toll the bell,
& that nobody see my dead body, & that no
mourners come to my funeral,
& that no flowers be planted on my grave,
& that no man remember me.
To this I put my name.   *Michael Henchard*

"What should we do?" asked Donald.

Elizabeth could not answer at first. "Oh, Donald!"
she said at last through her tears. "What bitterness
lies there! I would not mind so much, if I had not
been so unkind at our last meeting."

Elizabeth-Jane tried to do just as Henchard had
asked in his will. She knew that the man who had
written those words meant what he said.

All was over at last, even Elizabeth-Jane's regrets.
The years passed, and she and Donald shared a
happy, peaceful life together. Elizabeth-Jane spent
her time helping those who were less fortunate. She
felt that she deserved everything she had, but she
also knew that other people had less than they
deserved. Her youth had taught her that happiness
was but a rare moment in a general drama of pain.